#23

Antionette M. Courts

LIFE LESSON

Copyrights

Life Lesson

Copyright © 2025, Antionette Marie Courts

All rights reserved. No part of this publication may be

reproduced, stored in a retrieval system or transmitted in any form

or by any means, electronic, mechanical, photocopying, recording

or otherwise, without prior written permission from the publisher,

Engraving Your Views. All rights, reserved, including the right to

reproduce this book or portions thereof in any form

ISBN Hardcover:

9798998638909

Ebook:

979899863896

LCCN:

2025907717

Dedication

To my grandmother,

I dedicate Lessons learned to you. You raised me in church

which taught me to trust God. Your strength showed me nothing

was too difficult to conquer. I realize life was easy raising your grandchildren on your own but we never were never neglected.

You provided for us; your strength made me strong; your

knowledge made me wise. Because of the sacrifices you made I learned how to make the little I had to be enough.

Grandmother

you were the bravest and strongest Woman I have ever known. I will always love you.

To my sons,

I dedicate this book to both my sons.

From the moment I held you in my arms, I knew I would love you

both forever. Both of you showed me being vulnerable wasn't a sign of weakness and although we don't agree on everything, you both have always respected me. I am proud to be called your mother. Now as men I see your destined for greatness.

My world wouldn't be complete without you.

To my daughters,

I dedicate this book to you, each of you has taught me many things throughout your childhood but the most important has been confidence.

As I've watched you grow to be strong beautiful black women, I see my lessons in life were not in vain. Each of you are independent, and

intelligent. All of you have encouraged me to write this book not in words but in the ways I see myself in you. You're my joy and you've showed me to enjoy life

To my daughters,

I dedicate this book to you, each of you has taught me many things throughout your childhood but the most important has been confidence.

As I've watched you grow to be strong beautiful black women, I see my lessons in life were not in vain. Each of you are independent, and

intelligent. All of you have encouraged me to write this book not in words

but in the ways I see myself in you. You're my joy and you've showed me to enjoy life.

To my grandchildren,

I dedicate Lesson's learned to my grandchildren and great granddaughter, has show shown me what unconditional love feels like. They have taught me to be patient and enjoy the little things in life. I am blessed to have you in my life.

To my cousin and his wife

I dedicate this book to you on so many levels, but most importantly, you showed me what true love looks like. Neither of you always kept it real, you were always there supporting me and when I didn't you the most, thank you. Neither of you always kept it real, you were always there supporting me and when I didn't you the most, thank you.

Table of Contents

.... Error! Bookmark not defined.

Dedication 3

Chapter 1 8

In the Beginning 8

Chapter 2 16

Tell me if you love me. 16

Chapter 4 30

Motherless 30

Chapter 5 34

First love 34

Chapter 6 41

The grass isn't always greener on the other side. 41

Chapter 7 48

The proposal 48

Chapter 8 58

Get away plan 58

Chapter 9 65

The Divorce 65

Chapter 10 71

Loss 71

Chapter 11 76

The Funeral 76

Chapter 12 83

Chapter 13 86

Near death experience 86

Chapter 1

In the Beginning

It's hard to know where to start, so let me start at the beginning from what I remember. I was an only child for six years, living in the project, Henry Horner Homes in Chicago, with my grandmother and mom, which I was never allowed to call mom, I could only call her by her first name, which sounds ridiculous, but true. I'll explain why later. Our apartment had two bedrooms, a kitchen, and a living room. I slept in the same room as my grandmother because she had two beds, and mom slept across the small hallway in the other bedroom.

We didn't have much money, but I was always clean, and there was always something to eat. My grandmother cleaned white people's houses for a living, and my mother went to medical school. Sometimes, when I didn't have school, I would accompany my grandmother to her job. Those were fun days because the owner had two daughters, and one of the girls was about the same age as me. Being black didn't matter to me because I was never taught that I was different and should know my place; that changed one day when we were outside the house playing, and she called me her black baby doll to her friends. That was the day things changed. I didn't say anything until my grandmother, and I got home; I didn't understand then that she didn't see me as her equal.

That evening, I told my grandmother what happened, and she sat me down before mom came home and told me that wouldn't happen again because I wasn't returning. It felt like a punishment; she never went into detail, but I could tell she wasn't happy about the situation.

My grandmother and mother were born in the West Indies, Virgin Islands, and were very independent women. I never knew my father, and you can't miss what you never had, or can you? At that time, it didn't make a difference cause most kids I knew didn't have a dad around either. All the women in my life were always self-reliant, and I was brought up the same way; I had never seen them ask a man to do or give them anything. They were both aggressive when handling situations; they got the job done.

In March of 1968, I was six years old when my brother was born; I remember my mom and grandmother rushing off to the hospital and allowing a male neighbor to watch me, something my grandmother would never do if given a choice. I'm not sure how old he was, but he was much older than me, maybe by twenty years or so. It was a basement apartment that had rats that would climb on the stove at night when the lights were out. I would be so scared that I would curl up like a ball and pull the covers over my head. The babysitter slept on the couch, he must of been used to the same thing in his apartment. I asked the babysitter if he could keep the light on in the kitchen. He said yes, and I was initially glad.

I'll call him Tony because I can't remember his real name. Tony was always friendly and helpful; maybe that's why my mom chose him to watch me. I had never feared him before, but this night was different; after he turned on the light in the kitchen, he said I could sit on the couch and watch television with him until I got sleepy. I was glad because I wouldn't be in the bedroom alone. I would've stayed in bed alone if I had known his intentions.

Once I sat on the couch, he started touching me all over. I asked him to stop, but he acted like he didn't hear my words. After that night, I would never be the same little girl again. I remember hurting and bleeding in my private area, and my pajamas had blood on them, too. Two days later, my mom came home with my baby brother, and I was so happy to see her and my grandmother. I wanted to tell them what happened right then, but they were so occupied with the new baby that I just kept quiet. Still hurting, when I finally told my grandmother what happened, she said," I will take care of it," and it was never brought up again.

After several days, everything was back to normal, at least on the surface. I realize life experiences are only challenges that make us stronger mentally and spiritually, but nothing would be the same for me. I was confused and depressed before I even knew what depression was; from that moment on, I never trusted anyone. How could they allow this to happen to me, and what happened to him for violating me? We never talked about it. I never went to the doctor or anything. Wasn't I important enough to protect. I'll never know the answer to that question. There's a lot I don't remember from that time in my life except my dislike of my brother for getting the attention I never got. I know now it was never his fault.

Several months have passed, and we are back at the projects and adjusting to the new baby; I thought having a brother to play with was cool. At least it meant I wouldn't be alone anymore. Mom was so happy with the baby, and she let me help feed him and rock him to sleep. Those days were great, and Mom spent a lot of time at home, which made things even better.

One morning, when my grandmother went to work, and I was home with my mom, she took me to the neighbor's apartment two doors down from where we lived. Our neighbor was a woman who had several children that I knew and played with from time to time. On this day, my mom asked the lady if she would take me because she had to leave. I thought she meant to leave for a little while and she would be back, but she was trying to give me away. Why would my mom want to give me away to a total stranger? Back in the sixties and seventies, you would not be allowed to drop your baby off at the hospital or fire station like there is today.

Our neighbor, whose name I can't remember, said no, so Mom took me back to the apartment with my brother and left. Soon after, grandmother came home from work and saw we were alone in the apartment. We heard a knock on the door, and when she opened the door, it was the neighbor whose mom had tried to give me away, too. Grandmother was distraught; she was so upset she started talking fast, and her face was even redder than usual. My brother and I were in the living room playing on the floor, making sure we stayed out of her way; it was funny because she wasn't mad at me. Our mom started staying away more and more. Sometimes, I thought she would never return, but she always did, and grandmother would start fussing again.

As a child growing up, I don't recall my grandmother ever using a babysitter to care for us when she had to work, maybe because of what happened to me years before. Grandmother's love wasn't hugs and kisses; she showed love by providing and making sure we had what we needed. Mom and grandmother kept us in clean clothes every day;

if our clothes were too big, she would sew them to make them fit; she showed me how to sew just about everything by hand and with the aid of her sewing machine. Cooking was no different; if grandmother was in the kitchen, so would I.

When enough is too much

How do you determine what's too much if you've never had enough of something? This has always puzzled me when I hear someone say they've had enough of this or that in their life; does that mean they didn't have enough before? Could it mean we don't know what's enough or not regarding matters of our lives? I have concluded that my life is enough and much more than I give it credit for and not enough that I would give it up.

Chapter 2

Tell me if you love me.

Grandmother was always in control of everything, so when she spoke, you didn't dare say a word; it didn't matter your age. My mom just stood there and took it. It was always that way. Many days after that, I was told to watch my brother when my grandmother went to work, and there were strict rules not to go outside. One day, I disobeyed that rule and took my brother to the playground. I told my brother not to say anything, or I won't take him to the playground anymore, and he promised, but as faith would have it, my brother fell off the stairs of the metal sliding board.

I was so scared when that happened for two reasons: one, because he started to have a big knot on his forehead, and second, I was going to get my behind beat, when my grandmother got home from work. I didn't know what to do for my brother; he wouldn't stop crying, but he wasn't bleeding.

When grandmother came home from work, and the moment she laid eyes on my brother, it was curtains for me. When she asked what happened, I didn't lie. I told her the truth after she tended to the black and blue lump on his forehead, and she immediately turned her attention to me with a butt whipping. I never did that again.

On Saturdays, my grandmother and I would go to confession after cleaning the church; I never saw the need to confess anything, as I was only nine. But because my grandmother was a devoured Catholic, we confessed religiously, no pun intended.

What I dreaded mostly was being made to tell a priest (man); I could never understand why we needed an interpreter to speak to God on our behalf. There were steps to this Saturday ritual.

1. The first would be to step into a small room that had a small screen window that slid side to side for talking.

2. Kneel and pray "Father forgives me for I have sinned.

3. Confess my sins for that week and wait for instructions to be forgiven

4. Lastly, the priest would tell me to say several Hail Mary's and light candles to be forgiven.

As a kid, I felt the Catholic church was hypocrites because, according to Matthew 21:12 in the Bible, "said Jesus went into the temple of God and cast out all of them that sold and bought in the temple and overthrew the tables of the money changers, and the seats of them that sold doves." Although they were selling doves, I feel bingo is the same thing; I know bingo wasn't played inside the church but still took place on church grounds. There were so many things I didn't agree with about the Catholic church.

My grandmother was heavily into the church; she also believed in witchcraft; my grandmother told me to hold a piece of newspaper between my teeth when I had to sew thing I still had o it would prevent me from sticking myself.

She showed me that I could walk on a person all day if they were harassing me by writing their name on a piece of paper and then placing it in the shoe that I would wear for the day. There are many superstitions she had me believe; for example, never throw your hair in the garbage because someone could use it against you; crazy, right? But I believed it, and to this day, I would burn the hair left in my brush or comb. When I got mad at anybody, I would put their name in both my shoes. I thought this was wrong, but I could go to confession and be forgiven, right? Not right. I believe this is how generational curse began.

If that wasn't enough, my brother and I attended Catholic pre-school; when I was seven years old, we moved out of Henry Horner projects into another project building on California and Roosevelt Road in Chicago, which is now called Roosevelt Square, on the twelve floor. I was happy that I didn't have to attend Catholic school anymore, and cleaning the new church wasn't as frequent, maybe because this new church called Saint Lucy was further away.

Being in public school was very different than Catholic school; we didn't have to wear uniforms, and it wasn't as strict, but making friends was hard at first because I talked with a strong accent, and the other kids would make fun of how I talked, although I was born in Chicago. Being in a household with my mom and grandmother, I couldn't help but speak with the accent. This would make me stand out from other kids at school. The teacher would constantly call on me to help pass out homework and run errands, this caused the other students to call me the teacher's pet and a nerd because I was very smart. But I wanted the other kids to stop calling me the teacher's pet, so I started acting out at school, which would be a butt whipping if mom or grandmother had to come up to the school, so that didn't happen too often.

Being educated was a prerequisite in our household, I was taught knowledge is everything to get ahead in life. My grandmother would except nothing below a B grade when it came to any given assignments. For every exam or assignment, I would become anxious even though I studied.

I remember twice getting a C grade on a math test and scared to let my grandmother know. But eventually she would find out, so I showed her the paper and got popped hard on the hand for not studying hard enough to get a better grade even though C was a passing grade.

She had very high standards when it came to education, she didn't talk much about her education except how far she had to walk to get there. Either way she was very knowledgeable when it came to self-preservation, grandmother taught us lessons that school could never teach. Grandmother would tell me she was made to work with her mother in the fields cutting down Sugar Canes. My mom graduated high school and gave birth to me in her senior year, I'm sure grandmother had a lot to do with her completing High school. My father, who was twenty-two, married my sixteen-year-old mother. I'm unsure what the laws were at that time, but I'm pretty sure grandmother had to approve the marriage. It's sad to say, I don't know a lot about my mother other than she was smart, beautiful and worked as a waitress at a small fast-food joint not far from home and attended a Medical Assistance school in the evenings.

When mom was at work, grandmother would allow me and my brother to play outside the apartment. Even though we lived on the twelve floor we were protected by the bars on all the balconies. I like the fact that mom and grandmother lived next door to each other, most of the time I would sleep over my grandmother's apartment and mom didn't mind, except the day grandmother washed and hot combed my hair.

I didn't know my mom would get upset so when I showed my mom how grandmother did my hair, she was instantly upset, I probably said it with attitude, I think she was upset because I didn't ask first. She was so mad that she hit me, and I fell into the big television on the floor. I started to cry and ran to my grandmother's apartment, but my grandmother made me go back to mom's apartment.

But I didn't go back to the apartment, I left the building and walked to the police station a couple blocks away. I told them what happened, and they took me to my mother's apartment, my grandmother was there too. Both were worried and upset because I was nowhere to be found. They asked my mom what happened, and she told them exactly what had happened, since the police said it was an accident that I fell against the television there was no need for a report.

Then my mom surprised us all when she said, "since she wants my mother to do ever thing for her, she can stay there if she wants to". The police asked me in front of both who did I want to live with, and I quickly answered; my grandmother, and from then on, I lived in grandmother's apartment with all my belongings.

Things seemed to be better between me and my birth mom, she talked to me more nothing serious but for her to laugh with me gave me joy, more than she would ever know. I remember playing double Dutch outside and she jumped rope with me; that was a great day. All of us would eat at grandmother's apartment when she cooked a lot. One day she made liver and onions over rice, but I wanted nothing to do with that and didn't eat it, grandmother told me if I didn't eat it I was not going to eat that night, quiet as kept that was perfectly ok with me.

Other dinners were great, especially grandmother's greens with Red Snapper fish with rice.

Some nights after dinner grandmother and mom would play cards and me and my brother would be playing in the next room until it was time for bed. Other times mom would have her boyfriend come over, but she never let him spend the night around us. At that time, we had no idea that her boyfriend was my brother's father. He was tall and soft spoken he was always nice to my brother and me. One night they got into a big argument and mom would curse him out she even threatened to shoot him, so he left and stayed away for a long time.

Then there was a guy who started coming around to see our mom and he was big and tall and would give my mom anything she wanted. He was always nice to me and my brother. Me and my brother would laugh when he came over because he had such a huge head.

On the night of July 1972, I remember waking up from a bad dream, I dreamed that my mother was on fire and screaming but nobody would help her, and she died. I told my grandmother about my dream, and she told me to pray about it and that all dreams aren't always about the person you dreamt about. I was afraid my dream would become reality, but I prayed like grandmother said and felt everything would be ok. As time moved on, I didn't worry about it much because everything was going great. Mom was happy plus me and my brother were getting along, and I felt it was only a matter of time that mom would say she was proud of me, and give me a big hug, because I always brought home good grades from school except for the C in math. Unfortunately, that day would never come.

Chapter 3

Nothing lasts forever

It seemed at first like a movie that turned into a nightmare. Nothing could prepare me for the morning of August 1972. I remember my grandmother telling me to get ready to go with her to church; this was her day to help at the church, but I always tagged along. My brother was six years younger than me but got to stay home with mom; my brother was her favorite child and could do nothing wrong. My mother was 17 years old when she became pregnant with me. I never seen my dad around, it was always my mom and grandmother and sometimes my brother's dad would come around. I loved my mother, but I never felt she loved me back, I wasn't allowed to call her mom around other people only by her first name, something I would never allow my children to do. People thought we were sisters because she was young, and I looked just like her.

My mother was so pretty to me, she was tall and shapely, not fat or skinny, just perfect and I wanted to look just like her when I grew up. I always imagined my mom spending time with me, but most of all to hear her say I love you. Unfortunately, she would never get the chance.

I recall the weather was hot and someone had opened the water hydrant for us Kids to get wet, and girls were jumping rope downstairs at the playground. I was able to play double duce but not for long because I would be helping grandmother at the church. We stayed at church long enough for grandmother to clean the pews and vacuum the rugs. It seemed like we were there for hours before we finally left to walk home. I was happy that it wasn't late because I could stay outside and play until dinner was ready. Before we got close to our building, we saw smoke and heard the fire trucks and police sirens. I could've never imagined that my world would never be the same.

Grandmother and I were maybe only a block away when kids from the neighborhood were running up to me saying "your mom jumped out the window like superwoman";

hearing that made me run toward our building, I didn't realize our apartment was on fire. Our apartment was on the 12th floor I didn't understand what was going on at the time, all I could see was smoke coming from the 12th floor. I knew something was wrong; I wanted to know if the kids were kidding when they said my mom jumped out the window.

They had to be lying because no way mom would leave my brother in a burning house and certainly not jump out of a twelve-story window.

There were so many people at the building, a lot of fire trucks and police present, the entry to the building was restricted. Grandmother asked one of the police officers was anybody hurt; before he answered that question, he asked her if she lived on the 12th floor at the end of the hall. I was so scared that something bad had happened to my brother and mom; could this be the dream I had a month ago .

One of the officers drove my grandmother and me to the hospital where they took my mom. When we got to the hospital grandmother told me to wait in the waiting area with another police officer, from where I was sitting, I could see a Chaplin from the hospital was talking to my grandmother. She went with the Chaplin an one police officer, which seemed like hours but was only minutes before she returned, she wasn't crying so maybe mom was alright and my brother was too.

But that was far from the truth, my life would never be the same and my whole world was turned upside down, when grandmother said to me that my mom died in the fire. Grandmother confirmed that mom fell or jumped we would never know how; at that moment I felt like someone had snatched my heart right out of my chest. I asked what about my brother and she said he was in another hospital for children with smoke inhalation, but he would be ok. Somehow, that didn't make me feel any better; all I could do was cry.

Later I found out from reading a newspaper article that two armed men with a container of gasoline knocked on the door of the apartment. When my brother opened the door, one of the men wanted money, and she didn't have any, so he doused her with gas and lit her on fire; this had to be speculation because how would they know if they won't there? The only person that knew anything was my four-year-old brother, who was too young to testify. My brother was hospitalized for three months at Saint Anthony's Children's Hospital.

 The Red Cross helped us by finding a temporary shelter and some emergency services to help us get by. Much of my memory is foggy after the trauma of losing my mother. I had always seen my grandmother as a mom than a grandmother, but now she would be my mom forever. I didn't know what to do with all my emotions except cry and be angry. I would never understand how another human being could be so cruel to take another person's life and how could I forgive him. I couldn't put his name in my shoes because I didn't know it, and all the witchcraft in the world couldn't bring my mom back.

Chapter 4

Motherless

Grandmother was so strong, and I never saw her shed a tear, but maybe not in front of me. I was never that strong, especially now. I believe if I didn't have post-traumatic stress disorder after being violated by the babysitter, I sure as hell have it now.

 Some time passed and we left the shelter and moved in with my aunt. She worked at the same hospital where they took my mom, my aunt was pretty and smart, she had a son who was in the military, whom I met only once. She lived in a high-rise apartment where many nurses and teachers connected with the hospital stayed.

Her apartment was small but adequate for one person, not three. My aunt considered herself the black sheep of the family, but I never understood why. She was very fair skinned with light brown hair; she could pass for white if she wanted, and so could grandmother. My aunt looked much like my grandmother when she was young.

Unfortunately, staying with my aunt proved to be a huge mistake; even though her sister had just died, and her mother was still grieving the loss of her youngest child, she treated us like strangers. We were made to sleep on blankets between the bathroom and closet; it almost felt like she was punishing us for the death of my mom.

But it was about my aunt's relationship with her mother. Grandmother was very straightforward with her words and actions; maybe it was the way grandmother was raised. I remember one morning grandmother's chest was hurting and she was short of breath, and I didn't know what to do, my aunt said she was faking, and she would be ok, but she wasn't and 911 had to be called, I was scared I would lose her too; that I couldn't take.

If sleeping on the floor wasn't enough, it seemed so harsh whenever she spoke to grandmother. I was confused about it all. Why was this all happening? I became bitter and angry about everything and everybody. Why was nobody telling me how my brother was doing? Why did God let this happen? I was angry with God.

I didn't want to go to church anymore; I didn't want to pray. I thought praying and being faithful to church would save you from the bad stuff; We were going to church, confessing our sins, praying, lighting damn candles and He still took my mother away.

I was nine years old, and my world was falling apart. The first lesson of many for me was that nothing is forever.

Grandmother has always been the bravest woman I've ever known, but I could see the sadness in her eyes. She taught me to be brave and depend on God in all things. Even in this situation, I never saw her cry; she stayed focused, making all the arrangements for my mom's funeral. I remember the funeral home was packed with family and friends of mother and grandmother to show their support.

I was still angry at the world; now there was no chance for her to say she loved or hugged me. How could the world be so cruel? Why would anyone want to kill my mom or brother? It wasn't until age ten, when I asked God to forgive me and help me overcome these difficult times. We all needed some therapy to help us cope.

Time has passed, and I'm now a teenager and still dealing with the loss of my mom, but life circumstances somehow have a way of forcing us to rely on God for answers that nobody else can answer. My brother was doing well, and we moved from my aunt's apartment to a lovely courtyard apartment on the second floor.

We both attended public school and walked to school with other neighborhood children; I was starting to feel better. We even started going back to church, but I no longer had to go to confession. I started a journal to release the anxiety I was feeling inside; I didn't need confession for the pain I was going through because I didn't believe sorrow was a sin.

I wasn't sure what I was feeling, and I didn't want to discuss it with my grandmother because I could see she was coping with her own pain in her own way. She would hum church songs all day and crochet; I think that's what helped her get through the day. No matter what grandmother was going through, she never lost sight of the importance of caring for my brother and me.

Chapter 5

First love

My grandmother taught me many things about life but not how to cope with loss. Especially at thirteen years old. Grandmother was very strict when it came to my brother and me; she would always tell me to lead by example because I was the oldest.

When I said strict, that was an understatement, I mean strict to the point she would check me to make sure I had my period every month. I recall being a couple days late; I knew I wasn't pregnant because I didn't have sex yet, but I was still afraid to say that I hadn't started yet. I tried to fool her by putting red fingernail polish on the sanitary napkin so when she checked it would look like I started. Grandmother was nobody's fool, that just made her mad and she still accused me of having sex, and she was not having it. I got my behind beat for lying about it and trying to be slick about it. The kind of beating with a whole lecture behind it. Luckily, days later I really started but there was never an apology from her for the whipping she gave me; honestly, I really deserved it for lying.

As I got older, she stopped checking me every month, but that didn't stop her from accusing me of messing around with boys. But one day when she was away, curiosity got the best of me, so I told my boyfriend to come over; and yeah, you guessed it, I had sex but this time it was by choice. He was my first love, and I thought I was his. Once it was over we kissed, and I told him to leave before my grandmother and brother came back; I wasn't the only person afraid of grandmother, it seemed like everyone in the neighborhood was.

Back in the seventies children were respectful to all adults even if it wasn't your parent, and everybody in the neighborhood would respect grandmother even the guys that we called thugs.

When she sent me and my brother to the grocery store, which was about a half a mile away from our apartment, she would sit in the window and watch until we returned.

I would try to go over to my boyfriend's house every time she asked me to go to the store. I never had a problem going to the store but I had to play it cool so she wouldn't suspect I was going against her rules.

I really liked him, and he liked me too; but my grandmother would never allow me to have a boyfriend, so I sneaked to see him every chance I got. I could never even have girls over because grandmother didn't trust anyone. I guess that's why I don't trust people enough to call them my friend. My grandmother didn't suspect we liked each other; we were in the same class at school also the same marching band after school. I first met him at the YMCA one summer during swimming classes, he wore bi-focal glasses, nerdy and he wasn't even handsome, but he was so smart especially in math, and he made me laugh, he was differently my kryptonite.

He said I was pretty, and he liked the way I talked. Any time I was allowed to go outside I would have to take my brother with me, that made me mad sometimes because I knew he would always tell her. Even though he would get on my nerves at times I reminded myself that I almost lost him in the fire too.

When I was fifteen years old, I would ask about my father, she would say he was no good, but she never told me why, but in fact he had married my mother before I was born. I'm pretty sure grandmother had a lot to do with him not coming around to be in my life. She always would talk negative when it came to any man in my mother's life, and it was no different when it came to me. I would say to myself of course that I couldn't wait to get grown so I could go away and do whatever I wanted.

Don't get me wrong, grandmother was having fun at times too, we would go out to the movies some Saturdays, downtown Chicago on the bus: back then we could buy a city bus ticket that lasted all that day. Grandmother would even sneak food and snacks in her big purse, stuff like white Castle burgers, small juices and candy too, after the movies we walked to Ronny's Steakhouse located just a block away for a late lunch. Grandmother would let me stay up with her to listen to late night radio; not music but mystery stories or scary stories, I think that's how I started liking scary movies.

During this time my uncle retired from the military with a purple heart and many awards and metals, he was still humble and soft spoken, he never talked about his experience in the Army, and even though I knew he had to get hurt bad to receive a purple heart; I wanted to be just like him. This time when our uncle came to visit, he was married, and his wife was pregnant.

She was very beautiful with long black hair. She didn't speak much English, but she was nice to me and my brother. Grandmother would say my uncle treated her like a queen because all she did was sit in the window all day. I could not understand why grandmother had a problem with her.

They stayed with us for a short while, then they moved nearby and would visit now and then. I loved my uncle like a father since I never met my father, he didn't do anything special like a dad,

but at least he was available. I was in high school, and my brother was in middle school, I couldn't wait to graduate so I could go to college and become an attorney. My goal was to be a defense attorney; maybe I could make a difference "I was young it seemed like a great idea.

I graduated early in my Junior year from Josephinum High School. I had to catch two buses to get to school I was back in Catholic school, but I didn't have to wear a uniform like elementary school.

We never owned a car, and my grandmother never drove, we either walked or caught the bus which was right across the street from our apartment. As soon as I graduated, I applied to a four-year college, my major was a Criminal law, my alternate class was French.

I was doing great in Criminal law but horrible in French. I never wanted to take a bad grade home, so I dropped the class and took Spanish as an alternate. I did much better in Spanish, compared to failing every quiz and test in French. Eventually, I quit after the first semester.

I decided I wanted to leave home all together and travel the world; but I was only seventeen without a job. I just knew I wanted something different for my life than what I had.

Although I have tried many alternatives to Christ, only to return home again with Christ leading my way often feeling like I'm grabbing on to the hem of His garment. As a teen, I had been through so much already, losing my innocence and losing my mom, but I still had my grandmother, and that was everything to me. Although I loved her, I didn't want to be under her strict rules. I don't want to sound ungrateful because I'm not; I appreciate my grandmother teaching me how to be an independent young lady, but I wanted to experience the world, and I would never be able to do that at home.

Chapter 6

The grass isn't always greener on the other side.

I have done many things that didn't include Christ, and leaving home was one of them. Before leaving college, we had career day, and many companies presented their specialties. Still, one organization piqued my interest because it involved leaving home and making money simultaneously. Plus, the biggest bonus was I got to travel for free, and that was the United States Army.

There was only one problem I had to be eighteen to join and I was only seventeen at the time, so I would have to get grandmother's permission to get into the delayed entry program. This program lets you take the written test and physical test and if I passed everything; when I turned eighteen, I could be part of the program. That presented another problem, my grandmother would never sign for me to leave home. I knew this would be hard trying to convince her that this was a positive move, and I could better support the household by serving in the Army.

At first, she was not in agreement, but I didn't give up hope that she would change her mind before my eighteenth birthday. There I was on my knees praying by the beside at night begging God to grant me favor and let her sign me up for the Delayed entry program. Days went by without a word from her about signing, I was starting to get anxious and thinking I would never be able to leave if grandmother had anything to do with it.

It was two weeks before my eighteenth birthday, when she agreed to let me go but could see she wasn't happy about it. She felt I was abandoning her and my brother, that was further than the truth, I just wanted to live my life and staying home made me feel trapped. Two days later we called the recruiter, and she granted me permission to leave. I was so excited and anxious at the same time not knowing what to expect, I had never been away from home except when my eight-grade class went to Springfield. That night all the recruits stayed at the Roosevelt Hotel in downtown Chicago and the following day we would all start thirteen weeks of basic training.

We have already been assigned to our permanent duty station according to our score on the placement test we took. My duty station was going to be Germany. I was ecstatic and couldn't wait, but I had to pass basic training, which involved vicious physical and psychological training. I had never run track or done push-ups.

Every morning, we were woken up at the crack of dawn, and I do mean dawn, at three in the morning, to run a mile and then do sit-ups and push-ups. I was horrible at push-ups. Before a shower we were taken to breakfast as a platoon and before you entered the chow hall, we had to use the monkey bars and if you didn't make it to the end you would have to go to the end of the line, there were many times I had to go to the back of the line. I didn't think at first that I would pass training because I couldn't do pushups, and to pass basic, I had to do at least twenty-five pushups, fifty sit-ups, and run a mile in under eight minutes. I didn't have a problem with the sit-ups or running but those damn pushups were another story. I asked some of the other girls how I could do better at doing a pushup, and they told me the only way to do pushups is to do pushups; so every night before lights out, I would practice doing pushups until I had it down packed.

You're probably saying to yourself, "OK, that's physical, but what's psychological?" You need to realize there will be a Drill sergeant in your face yelling, trying to intimidate you daily. This didn't bother me; it was comical, and it didn't scare me. It did make one of the drill sergeants mad. I was accustomed to being yelled at by my grandmother, so I was already conditioned.

Our Drill sergeant would stand before me and stare me down to see if I would blink first, but he lost every time. Whenever that happened, he would make me do stupid stuff like tell a tree that I loved it repeatedly until he got tired, but I never broke.

I enjoyed basic training for the most part because I was away from home, surrounded by other girls and guys who were working toward a common goal to graduate basic training, better known as Boot camp. I was enjoying my newfound freedom. Each Boot camp Platoon had a title. I was in Charlie Company. We would sing cadence every time we marched or ran. The boot camp was in New Jersey, and you couldn't leave unless you had a pass for the weekend.

On most free weekends, we would go bowling or see a movie on post. Everything was in the post except for a mall. We had a laundry mat, barbers, a hair salon, a movie theater, a bowling alley, a small store that sold stuff like underwear, writing paper, envelopes, stamps, junk food, and even a night club. I was experiencing life like never before.

We took our physical training test at the end of thirteen weeks, and I passed, barely doing twenty-five pushups. I was promoted to Private first class, and graduation was scheduled the following week. I was proud of myself—I had made it. My brother and grandmother came to my graduation, which made me very happy.

I wish mom were here to share my joy. Mom, I miss you so much; sometimes it hurts. If you were still here with me, I would care for you and make sure you were happy every day because I love you. There wasn't much time between graduation and my next duty station, so we were given one week's leave to return home and spend time with our family. Fort Lee, Virginia, was my training facility, where I was trained as a material supply specialist (MOS) military occupation specialist. I now have much freedom to hang out every weekend unless I am assigned a duty for that weekend, but I could always find someone to swap duties with so I would be free. This was a new experience, doing what I wanted and living life. There was a female in my platoon with whom we had become friends; we would go places and watch each other's back.

She was from Cleveland, Ohio. We would go to the mall off-post and party together. There was always a party at one of the hotels near post, and if we didn't get too rowdy, management had no problem with us. The guys would always try to be with us, but we would hold out unless he were someone we liked. I held out for a long time but was free to do whatever I wanted, if I wanted.

I didn't know it at the time, but there was a guy always hanging around asking about me. He was very easy on the eyes, I must say, and I was attracted to him. When we finally were introduced, I learned that he was born in Hawaii. After a month of hanging out together we planned to get a room at the Hotel where everyone would party. I made sure to tell my friend what room we were in and she did the same. I was nervous but ready for whatever, but I was surprised when he said he didn't believe in sex before marriage. We were only nineteen at the time. That made me like him even more, but what was he saying? Did he want to marry me?

I had never been told that before, which was hard to process. Was he, my prince? Would he be my true love? Ok, girl, wake up; life is not a fairy tale. I had to snap myself back into reality. I couldn't marry him. I didn't even love myself, let alone love someone else.

Chapter 7

The proposal

I had to tell the only friend I had what he said, and she was as surprised as I was when he said it. The question was, if he asked me to marry him, what would I say? Days went by and he hadn't said anything about marriage, so I thought he was only saying that because he really did find me attractive, or maybe he changed his mind because I hung around a lot of the men in the unit, but they would just guy friends that made me laugh and not boyfriends.

I didn't think much of it because we hardly knew each other. On our early morning run, my friend fainted, and the ambulance took her to the hospital. I was so worried because she didn't return. I asked my instructor about her condition and was told she wouldn't be coming back and that she had a heart condition.

My best and only female friend was gone; who would I share gossip with now? I was confused and sad. I was confused because we ran every day, and she had never fainted before, but she did take pills. I thought the pills were prescribed, and how did she pass the physical intake with a heart condition? Something wasn't adding up, but she wouldn't be coming back. Training would be over soon, and then we would be shipped off to our main duty stations to do the job we were trained for. I was surprised on our last training day when the prince asked me in my story to marry him; he had a ring, too. Silly me, I said yes, I wasn't even twenty, yet I was about to become somebody's wife. I didn't even tell grandmother about the big event that would take place in my life.

To give you the back story, in the military, if you are married, they are supposed to station both of you at the place to continue your service; unfortunately, that was not the case for us. We married in San Antonio, Texas, where his uncle was an ordained minister. We even consummated our marriage on our short honeymoon. Since we were married, we thought the Army would change our orders to the same place, but like I said before, that never happened, so he stayed in Texas, and I left for Germany; our tour of duty would last three years. This was the first lie of many to come from the military. We weren't happy about the situation, but we couldn't do anything to change it. We called each other every chance we got and wrote letters.

My job there was easy; I would fix communication radios for the infantry unit and transfer them to their proper Battalion. As time passed, my husband and I spoke less and less because we were busy doing other things, some good, some bad. While in Germany, I met a soldier older than me, and we hit it off. He was certainly more experienced than me, and one thing led to another. I was so naïve that all his smooth talking got me right where he wanted me in his sheets. I was not proud of my actions, but I soon found out I was pregnant with his child. Now, I had to tell my husband I was pregnant with another man's baby. I knew that would probably break his heart, but I had to tell him.

I called my husband and told him the news of my pregnancy; he was silent for seconds; after the silence, he surprised me by saying he still wanted me, and we could raise the baby together, but I told him I would never feel right. We should get an annulment since nobody knew we consummated our marriage. He agreed after I said the baby's daddy was in the picture. Why couldn't I get pregnant after consummating our marriage? That was a question nobody could answer.

I felt I did the right thing by letting him free from me. But how could I tell my grandmother I was having a baby when I didn't even let her know I got married, and now I'm having another man's baby? I had to tell her sooner than later because it was getting more prominent as the months rolled by. My baby's father accompanied me to at least three prenatal exams. The other times, he was in Stugart working at his training job. We would be together when he wasn't in the field; I was still active at my job for eight months. We rented an apartment off-post; it was amicable and located near the Rhine River. He was very loving; he told me I could get out of the military, and he would take care of me and his child. Everything was happening so fast, at least in my head. What was I doing? I was running from one thing to another. My baby's father was from Puerto Rico, with curly black hair. Although his teeth were crooked, he had the biggest smile. He was much older than I mentioned before and ranked as a Sergeant first class.

I was now twenty years old, but I would be twenty-one when I was scheduled to give birth. He assured me that he would marry me, and I believed him; what a sucker. The following day, I spoke to my commanding officer and requested to be discharged to raise my child, but my commanding officer was reluctant to grant my discharge. He suggested I stay in, and there was help for soldiers with children, but I didn't believe that, so I insisted on getting out.

I was granted an honorable discharge because I was having a baby, a condition for being discharged honorably. So now I'm living off-post in a one-bedroom apartment near the river with a German landlord who barely spoke English. The landlord and her husband were very friendly. The wife would invite me to their place, which was directly upstairs from our apartment, for dinner. She showed me how to infuse fruit with alcohol.

Some mornings, I would go to the bakery down the block and buy fresh pastries, then sit by the river; life was good. I would tell grandmother after I had the baby, after the annulment, and after marrying my baby's father. I had it all figured out, at least in my head. My annulment was finalized on September twenty-three; months before my due date in October. I knew nothing about having a baby other than what other mothers told me. I was anxious to see my baby's face and excited at the same time, from all the birth stories I had been told and how their backs would hurt, and feet would swell up, I had none of those symptoms except morning sickness, and that was in my first month of my pregnancy. I would crave Hershey's with almonds at least five times a week.

I imagined my baby would look like him or me; It was a strange feeling when my baby moved inside me. I would talk to my stomach and play music sometimes. I was scheduled to take an ultrasound on October twenty; I was twenty-one years old, and this ultrasound was scheduled to see what gender I was having and make sure all was well. We had no car so I would have to catch the bus which was right across the street from our apartment; I remember walking and feeling a lot of pain that would come and go I figured I ate too much the night before and needed to go to the rest room, but then the pain kept worst; I was scared that something was wrong. I was crying from the pain and bent over, holding my stomach. Luckily, the soldiers saw me and offered me a ride to the hospital, which was more than a mile away. The soldiers kept telling me to breathe and not push, but the pain was unbearable. When I arrived at the military hospital in Frankfurt, one of the soldiers got a wheelchair, and one hospital nurse rushed me inside. The nurse said the same thing the solider said: don't push; I asked her if there was something wrong with my baby, and then she asked me how many months I was, and when I told her nine, she calmly said, "Honey, the pains are called contractions, and that's normal". I was glad but still in pain. I remember feeling like I was going to throw up every candy I'd eaten throughout my pregnancy.

In the delivery room were two nurses; one was holding my hand, and the other was assisting the doctor. I was more nervous than ever; I was about to bring a little person into the world. As soon as the doctor came in and checked my cervices then told me to push. I probably pushed three times before I heard my baby cry. When the doctor said it was a girl, I was overjoyed and grateful that she was healthy. I asked them to call his work unit so that I could come to see our precious baby girl. I asked him not to tell him what gender our child was; I was exhausted and excited at the same time, waiting for him to see his daughter; she looked more like him than me, with a head full of curly black hair and light skin like him, too.

He arrived three days later from the field, and when he saw the baby, he was smiling from ear to ear. After washing his hands, he picked her up and kissed her on the cheek, then looked at me and had the nerve to say, "You had a girl, and you need to clean yourself up." Now, I may be

many things, but I am not slow. The minute he entered the room; he could see the pink bow the nurse put on her little ankle. He was so rude; how did he expect me to look? I just had a medium-sized watermelon squeezed through me. One of the nurses that helped me in delivery must have heard his remark and told me, "It's ok." She also showed me how I should breastfeed my baby, but that only lasted for four days because her little gums were painful.

The day came for me to leave the hospital with my beautiful baby girl. I tried to be happy, but I kept thinking of what he had said to me at the hospital. Every day with my baby was worth the morning sickness and sleepless nights. Maybe I'm strange because every day of my pregnancy, I was happy I had a little person in me that I could love unconditionally, at least the best I knew how.

I told myself I would never treat my daughter the way my mom and grandmother had raised me.

After her dad had gone to work, the landlord asked me to walk with her. She said that would be good for the baby and me, instead of just being indoors. I agreed that having someone to help me adjust to motherhood was nice. Some days were more complex than ever, especially when she would cry and didn't know what I needed to do to calm her down. I would rock her and sing songs I learned in elementary school, but she liked going outside the most. So, did I. She was my world, and nothing outside our world mattered except keeping her safe. I would watch her sleep many times. I would take her out of her crib and place her on my chest so I could feel her little heart beat next to mine. My baby's daddy started working later and later, even when he wasn't in the mountain on duty, and I started to feel like he was messing around.

One day, I decided to go into Frankfurt, and do a little shopping for me and the baby. When we got to the train station, I saw her daddy walking hand in hand with another female. I couldn't believe it at first, but it was him with that stupid grin; he pretended he didn't see me walking toward him. Before he could speak, I slapped him in the face. The lady he was with started to say something, but I cut her off and told him, " How could you just ignore me and your baby, his response was, "You have no paper on me." I couldn't tell you if I was more hurt than angry. I went back to the apartment and decided to leave with our baby; he didn't seem to want the baby or me.

Chapter 8

Get away plan

I had a problem with my plan. I had no money to leave; I was thousands of miles away from home. I knew he would return to field duty for at least a month, and I had to act fast if I wanted us to be gone before he got back. I would need plane fare and money for enough baby food and formula to implement my plan. At this time, our baby girl was almost one year old.

My plan would be first to let the landlord know what was happening, ask to keep the following rent, and not sit down with him before I leave. I prayed they would agree, and they did. Next, I needed to sell everything we brought together; that part was easier than I thought because most of his associates knew he was cheating on me and didn't agree with what he was doing either. The day came to put my plan in motion. When he left that morning, I sold just about everything: a beautiful mirror cabinet, our brand-new couch, all our kitchen wear, and much more. I thought about selling the bed and making him sleep on the floor, but I didn't. After selling everything and I had an entire month's rent, I was still seventy-five dollars short. I was desperate to come up with the money, so I contacted my cousin, the only person I trusted at the time to help me, and he sent me exactly what I needed to fly back home to the States.

His best friend came by the day we were leaving and offered us a ride to the Frankfurt airport. I asked him how he knew I was leaving and, more importantly, if my baby's daddy knew too. He assured me that he knew nothing about me selling everything or leaving. I wasn't sure if I believed anything he was saying, but then he said the weirdest thing and asked if he had come to Chicago. Would I marry him so we could be a family and he would help me with my daughter?

I thought if I didn't say yes, he would call her father and my plans would've been for nothing, so of course I never thought he would come to Chicago since his hometown was New York, so to make him think I believed him I gave him my address. I surprised my grandmother and showed up with my beautiful baby girl. At first, she and my brother called me a whore and of course I was shocked to hear those words come out of his mouth and even more shocked that grandmother didn't knock his teeth out, if that was me, I would be scooping myself off the floor. I said Never in your life will you call me out of my name again. A month after being home, I found an apartment in the same building, two stories above my grandmother's. A friend of my baby's father sent me a letter saying he had finished his tour of duty and was coming to Chicago. I still didn't believe him, but I gave him the benefit of the doubt and sent him my phone number. He arrived in Chicago a week later, so I kept my word and married him. Crazy right? We got married in the Catholic church where my grandmother attained. The ceremony felt like we were at a courthouse.

I wondered if this was how my mother had been married to my father. Now I am married, so I wouldn't shame my grandmother by having a child out of wedlock. I didn't feel married; I had no idea what a wife was supposed to do other than have his babies, keep a clean house, and cook for the family; that was all I had to give him. We started our marriage on a lie because I didn't love him. Hell, I didn't even know him on top of that. After several months in the marriage, he told me he couldn't have kids because of an accident he had as a child.

Although we finished our three-year obligation to the Army, we still had a six-year obligation with the Army reserves. These training exercises helped us to stay on top of the jobs we originally trained for.

Everything was going great; my uncle moved into the apartment just upstairs, and I would ask him for advice on just anything. Besides, he was like a father to me. It was time for us to find a job because Reserve pay wasn't enough to pay the bills. Luckily, I got a job at the Warehouse Club on the North side of Chicago and made pretty good money. My husband, on the other hand, hadn't found a job outside of the Army Reserves. Because I didn't know him, I paid for daycare for my daughter. My daughter and I spent time with my grandmother and my brother and would often go to church with them, too, but we never went to confession. My daughter was baptized at my grandmother's church, and my cousin and his wife were the godparents.

I realize that being married is a commitment to each other, but if I were honest with myself, I wouldn't know what marriage is all about. As time went on, we resembled a real married couple. If I were on the outside looking in, I would think we were not made for each other. He was Cuban, short with hair like Castro; I don't even like short men.

When winter passed in 1982, my daughter was two years old, and we all moved, and so did grandmother, my brother, and my uncle, to Hammond apartments in Indiana. Of course, they were in separate apartments but close to each other. I found a new job as a sales representative for a company that sold Air purifiers and vacuum cleaners. I discovered I had a niche for sales; it was fun, and the money was good. As I mentioned, I would take my little girl to my great-grandmother at work. I liked my job because I didn't have to work long hours unless I chose to.

My husband: Our marriage was a great game of charades that I was losing badly. He started drinking and smoking, which is another strike in my book, especially around my daughter. I never saw him smoke before we got married. I started resenting everything about him; the only work he had to do was his obligation to the Army Reserves.

One weekend during his training away from home, I decided that my daughter and I would surprise him in Atlanta, Georgia, where he was doing his two weeks. I stayed in a hotel near the. On our second day at the hotel we went to see him but he was nowhere to be found; I asked some of the other soldiers in his unit did they know where he was and I was told he was in the laundry room and they would get him for me, I had a strange feeling they knew something more but wasn't going to spill the beans. I had no facts that he might be cheating on me like his friend did to me.

We waited in the day room where soldiers would go to meet family or recreation. When he finally showed up, my daughter ran over to him, and he picked her up and hugged us both with a kiss. I was glad to see him; we spent family time together before he returned to base. After two nights at the hotel, my daughter and I headed back home, and we would see him in a week when he returned home. When he came home, I cooked a nice steak and potatoes, mainly because baked potatoes were my baby girl's favorite. After dinner, we watched television until my little sweetheart fell asleep in my arms. The following day, I decided to wash clothes; it was customary to check all pockets before putting the clothes in the washer. When I checked the pockets of my husband's uniform pants, I found a note and photo; wow, that was bold of him to bring proof of his cheating, or maybe he didn't care if I saw it. The photo was of a girl from his platoon. On the back, it read, "I miss you already." I really didn't know why I was mad because I didn't love him, but I was, so I confronted him with the note. I asked him if she was the reason he took so long to come to the recreation room in Atlanta.

I don't know why I asked because anything he said would upset me. Although he said nothing happened, I wasn't stupid enough to believe that. From that point on I didn't care to be with him, I didn't cry like when my baby's father cheated on me, I was just pissed off because he could have stayed where he was before I married him if he still wanted to mess around with other women. I was partly to blame because I never should have married him.

Chapter 9

The Divorce

I became unfaithful and started liking one man who got my attention, even though I was still married. I didn't care about his feelings and became annoyed whenever I was around him. My daughter and I started spending more time around my grandmother and brother and less time at my apartment. One day at work, one of the guys asked if I could pick up his friend, who didn't have a car, for an interview for the sales position. I said yes.

When I arrived at his house, I was intrigued. He was handsome with brown eyes, dressed in a black velvet jacket and pressed dress slacks, and he smelled good. We talked on the way back to the job, and I found out he, too, was in the military as a Marine with an honorable discharge. He even had a daughter the same age as mine.

He got the job, and we teamed up selling; he was also good at his job. We drove the company's van to carry the equipment from house to house; we made a pretty good team. I started to like this man. I didn't care about my marriage. I even told him I was married, but I didn't know that sounded like a line everybody uses when they want to mess around. In this case, it was the truth. I realized the smart thing to do would be to divorce my husband. I never loved him anyway. I didn't care about his feelings anymore. I only cared about being happy. I found out this new guy was married and separated. We started seeing each other after work, and since his daughter was the same age as mine, I would take her for play dates with his daughter. They hit it off from the start. My husband, soon to be ex, spent the day smoking and getting high on weed.

One evening after work, a group from the job was going and wanted to go, and since my daughter was with my grandmother, I didn't think it would be a problem. I wouldn't use my car because I was getting a ride with the guy I liked and two other females from work. The group waited in the car as I climbed the stairs to my apartment to let the man I married that I was going bowling, he came outside on the balcony and looked to see who was in the car; before I knew it he slapped me across the face, the people in the car saw it, and the guy I liked stepped out the car and asked if I was alright, I'm pretty sure he had a feeling I was messing around with this guy. I said I was fine, they could go ahead without me, and I would see them at work tomorrow. When we stepped back into the apartment, he made it clear that if he couldn't have me, he would make it so that nobody else would. I could smell he had been drinking. Soon after he fell asleep, I sat in the kitchen watching him sleep, thinking if I killed him would I get caught, and decided against it. From that moment on, I remembered what my grandmother told me as a little girl: "If a man hits you once and gets away with it, he will do it again". He wasn't worth going to jail for, so the following day when he woke up, I made breakfast for him, then walked to my grandmother's apartment to get my daughter; I didn't dare tell my grandmother that my husband hit her because I would have to explain why. When I returned to our apartment, he was watching television; I sent my daughter to her room while making breakfast. While my daughter was eating, I sat next to him and told him I wanted a divorce. I knew he had no money, so I was ready to fly him to his family in New York. I didn't love the man, so why would I forgive him? he wasn't worth it. After I told him, he looked surprised that I wanted a divorce. Of course, he promised he would never hit me again and that he was just so mad and hurt. I told him I would never allow him to hit me again, so I insisted we needed to be divorced because I didn't love him from the start, and he had already cheated on me while at training. I told him we should've never gotten married. I don't think he believed I wanted a divorce, but he was sadly mistaken because I bought him a plane ticket back to his hometown in Brooklyn, New York, when I got paid. I drove him and my daughter to the airport that weekend and watched his plane take off. Now, all I needed

to do was file for divorce, and since I didn't know the address where he was going, I was granted the opportunity to post for our divorce in the law bulletin, and if there was no response in sixty days, I think- I'm not exactly sure- we would be divorced.

The year was 1984, and I was legally divorced. You would think I would've waited to start another relationship, but I didn't, and I continued seeing the guy from work. We were spending more and more time together, and at one point, my uncle, who was living right next door, asked if I knew what I was doing. Quite honestly, I had no clue; I was searching for something no man could give me: fulfillment and love. There was a void in my life, and I didn't know how to fill it. As our relationship grew, I allowed him to my apartment; he still lived with his mother. That should've been a red flag, but I overlooked it. I didn't feel comfortable with him sneaking me into the basement where he slept.

He started slowly leaving clothing items at my apartment each time he came over, and before I realized it, he had moved in. I finally introduced him to my grandmother, and she liked him. Grandmother would always say whatever was on her mind, whether you liked it or not; I think that's where I got it from because I do the same thing.

After about five to six months, we were living together, and my little girl liked him too, especially when he brought his daughter over. His daughter lived with his wife and his mother. He would often tell me that he was getting a divorce and would fight for custody of his daughter. Honestly, I didn't care if he got divorced or not since they were separated, and I had no intentions of getting married ever again. Meanwhile, I was looking for another job with stable hours and a salary.

I soon found a job as a billing clerk at Loretto Hospital on the west side of Chicago, which was exactly what I asked for. However, I forgot to ask God so my boss would not be prejudiced. My grandmother was still watching my daughter while I worked, and I would pick her up as soon as I got home.

I didn't know him enough to care for my precious little girl; I would never forgive myself if what happened to me happened to her. He would often drop me off and pick me up from work using my car, which was great because I would not have to worry about finding somewhere to park if the lot was crowded.

Chapter 10

Loss

About a year into our relationship, I discovered I was pregnant with his baby. He was happy, but I couldn't recognize joy from a stunned reaction. Since this would be my second pregnancy, I thought I knew what to expect, but I had no clue that each pregnancy would differ. I was in my first trimester, but didn't have an appetite and was always tired. One evening, when he was driving me home from work, I started having bad stomach pain. It felt like I had to do a number two, and when he pulled up to the apartment with his help, I made it to the bathroom. Unfortunately, it wasn't a bowel movement.

It was our baby that came out of me, and the pain was over. I started questioning myself: was I doing too much to cause the loss of our baby, should I have eaten more even though I wasn't hungry?

Nothing made sense as I stood in the bathroom watching the fetus of my baby flowing in the toilet full of blood. After standing there with tears in my eyes for hours it seemed, but it wasn't I yelled for him to come into the bathroom. He quickly came in. "What's wrong"? Before I could answer, he looked down to see our baby was no more.

He took our baby out of the toilet, which was so small, but you could see where the eyes were developing, and its little body was all curled up. He drove both me and our fetus to the nearest emergency room. It didn't take long before we were called back so I could see the ER doctor. My guy placed the towel on the desk in front of the doctor. The doctor didn't say anything we didn't already know. I had a miscarriage and needed a D & C. This would clean my cervix so I wouldn't get an infection, but I told the doctor everything passed with the baby, my body did its own D & C.

I cried all through the night. I didn't tell my grandmother or the uncle who lived next door; I just wanted to be left alone, including my guy. He didn't seem upset or sad; he was calm about everything. I should've seen the signs, but again, I didn't. Months have passed, and I've recovered from my loss physically, but mentally, it was a lot longer. I even went back to work. On Thursdays, some people from work would go bowling, and we would go with my baby girl. After one year and eight months of working at the hospital, I decided to quit but stayed on the bowling team.

It was raining heavily this evening, and I didn't feel like going bowling. I was tired and needed some sleep, so I let my uncle and brother use my car and took our places on the team.

We were all sleeping when the phone rang, and instantly, I knew something was wrong. The voice on the other end of the phone was calm. When she asked, "Is this Antionette?" I said yes. She told me there had been an accident. Before she finished the sentence, I asked, "Is everybody okay?" She only said we were working on the driver, and my brother was okay.

I don't remember dressing or taking my baby girl to her grandmother's apartment. We arrived at the hospital emergency room, where I met my brother, and I was taken to my uncle's room, where I identified his body.

The hospital sheet was draped over his body from head to toe. My chest felt like someone was standing on it and choking me at the same time. I was told my uncle died instantly due to the impact of the crash. He had died from his injuries before he got to the hospital. But my brother told me he didn't die right away, because my brother told me our uncle tried to talk to him but couldn't. The police report stated that while driving on the expressway, the car hydroplaned on the water from the rain and hit the guardrail, and my uncle broke his neck. I don't know if he was wearing a seat belt or not.

My brother wasn't severely hurt on the outside, but mentally, he had to be messed up. Now, how was I going to break the news to his mother that another child of hers was gone forever? First, my mother and now my uncle were her youngest children out of five. I was so conflicted about what to do first, call other family members to help me tell grandmother or tell her myself; I decided to tell her myself, the walk to my grandmother's apartment seemed like a mile even though it was less than a half a block.

My heart was beating so fast, and the tears wouldn't stop, but I did my best to hold it together. She must of known something wasn't right, I knelt in front of her sitting like a servant to a Queen, there was no easy or simply way to say it so with tears in my eyes I told her my uncle and brother were in a car accident and my uncle didn't make it; the pain of losing him will never go away because he was more than an uncle to me, he was a father figure in my life now there are two empty spaces in my heart mom and him. After I told grandmother, she said softly, "My son is gone? I knew she wasn't asking the question; it was just her realization that he was gone. Again, I can't say it enough: She will always be the strongest and bravest woman I've ever known, even to this day. Her next words to me were, "Get my address book." After that, I remember she called the church, and arrangements for his funeral were set. I was trying to hold it together, but every time I thought about the kind of man he was, I would break down in tears, and so did my brother.

Chapter 11

The Funeral

On the day of the funeral, so many people knew my uncle from his childhood, and as well as family, no dry eyes were sitting in church. The only people I expected to see but didn't were his wife and kids; although she was allowed to be there, she chose not to. It was hard to see my uncle in that brown coffin; I can't even remember what he was wearing; even as I write this book, it's tearing my heart apart just thinking about losing such a great example of a man in my life. The worst part of a funeral is going to the burial site. My uncle was an officer in the military with a purple heart medal, so at his burial, he had a shot gun salute, and if you've ever been to one, each shot would make your body jolt. Each shot brought back memories of him chillingly listening to jazz and the loss in my life.

The American flag was folded and given to grandmother while she sat quietly near my brother and me. For the grandmother, this would be the second time she would watch her child placed in the ground and say her final goodbyes. I will never understand why people say time will heal everything; it's a lie if you ask me. I think it's just something people say when they don't know what to say because this hole in my heart will never heal until I see their faces again. While all of this was taking place, I tried to explain to my daughter why Mommy was crying all the time. I was glad my daughter didn't understand the whole content of a funeral. After the funeral, friends and family members got together for a repass; this was something I never felt comfortable attending. I witnessed the burial of my mom. I disliked repass, who came up with this, a bunch of people you never even seen before gathering to eat and talk about the loved one who had just been buried.

I could never read my grandmother; if she was sad or happy, I could tell when she got mad. I know my brother was traumatized from the whole event since he was the one with him when he died. That event and the death of our mother- that's a lot. I don't think he will ever be the same; I wasn't there, and I will never be the same. I often wonder why bad things happen to good people. I consider my mom and uncle good people and love them both. Although I am no longer a child, I was feeling the same emotions I did as a child. I was not as strong as my grandmother when it came to holding back tears.

At this time, my guy was living with me and my daughter in Riverdale; we bought a house using a part of our military housing allowance. It wasn't fancy but adequate for the three of us and even big enough for his daughter to spend weekends with us. He was still married, but his divorce was in progress; the only holdup was the custody fight. I stayed out of his battle because it wasn't my battle to fight. He asked me for money to hire an attorney, thinking they could battle better in court than he could. It would cost ten thousand dollars to hire a law firm that specialized in getting father custody.

I was reluctant to lend him the money; you probably want to know why I had to apply for his loan. Mainly because his credit was a mess. I was approved, and he hired the lawyer.

On the day of the court, the judge left the decision up to his daughter because she was old enough to know who she wanted to live with. After the judge returned to the courtroom, the judge ordered that she stay in her mother's custody. Of course, he wasn't happy, but he was granted visitation rights.

I couldn't even begin to imagine how he felt about not getting custody of his daughter, but he had to respect the fact that his daughter wanted to live with her mother. It didn't matter what the ruling was; I still had a ten-thousand-dollar loan to repay. At first, he was giving me money to help pay off the ten-thousand-dollar debt, but as time passed, the help stopped due to his job situation, which left me paying off the debt. God gave me warning signs about this man, which I chose to ignore because I was in love with him. I wanted a family that included a mother and father raising our kids together, mainly because I didn't have the typical family dynamic growing up. Months later, he was hired as a computer technician in downtown Chicago. He was making a deceitful salary, and I was working as well. In 1985, I found out I was pregnant again, but this time, I had to quit working because I was at risk of losing the baby. My boyfriend ensured I was all right every morning before he went to work; I thought that was sweet of him.

In the afternoon, my boyfriend's childhood friend came by. he was the same person who had introduced me to him. I was upstairs when he rang the front doorbell, but I didn't rush to open the door because my guy was already downstairs. It had been some time before I started to come downstairs, but halfway down the stairs, I saw my guy quickly removing his hand from his friend's thigh, who was wearing shorts at the time. I did see what I saw, but the surprised look on my guy's face said it all, even though he denied it, and I let it go.

I knew his childhood friend was gay, but never would I believe my guy was on the down low. I could've ended the relationship right then and there, but again, I ignored the signs.

In March of 1986, I gave birth to a healthy baby girl. My guy was there for her birth and stayed by my side until they brought our baby to my room. He was so happy, with a big smile; I was happy too. After the three-day waiting period, I was discharged from the hospital with our baby.

Our baby girl favored her daddy more than me, so I'm glad he wasn't ugly; I'm just saying. We lived in the home until our baby girl was old enough to walk. Then, my guy wanted us to move closer to the city so that he would be closer to his mother, and I could have my grandmother live with us. She was getting older, and it was difficult for her to get around because her hips were always hurting. She was taking heart pills and a bunch of other medications; I wanted my grandmother with me so I could always take care of her. We moved into an apartment in Roseland near his mother, sister, and two brothers. I wasn't familiar with the area, nor did I have any family there except my cousin and his wife. The identical cousin who helped me when I needed seventy-five dollars to leave Germany with my baby. I will forever be grateful to both of them.

Another good thing was my grandmother. I was with my grandmother again; she started having trouble with her eyesight, and the Arthritis in her hands became more painful than usual. Grandmother loved to crochet, but the pain in her hands made it difficult. Her appetite decreased; she hadn't eaten much before, but now all she would eat in the morning was toast or saltine crackers with her favorite herbal teas, like honey and lemon or chamomile tea. When I tried to get her to eat more, she would refuse. Grandmother was still very spunky for her age; she would get under my skin some days, and other times, she was like a child. Our two girls attended school within walking distance from where we lived, and my guy and I had great work schedules; he worked days, and I worked nights at the hospital in downtown Chicago, so one of us would always be available to our grandmother and the girls.

We didn't work on weekends, which gave us time to spend together. We would let the girls go outside and play. My guy would pick up his daughter to spend the weekend, which was cool because she was the same age as my daughter, and they got along incredible, and I loved that. His daughter was respectful around me, so we had a good relationship. I enjoyed her company. When we took trips to Michigan to visit his older brother, we were able to take her with us, and we had a lot of fun. We also took her to Disney World one summer, along with our grandmother.

In 1987, he asked me to marry him again, and like before, I told him no; hell, I had been through this twice before, and it didn't work, so why would I do it again?

Chapter 12

The Sheep in Wolf Clothing

The year was 1987, and I thought this guy might be the one, but I still didn't want to give up my independence. I thought about what he said the last time I said no to his proposal, but kept thinking about whether I wanted to get married again, and my answer would always be no. I hoped he wouldn't ask me again because I was content with how things were. He was a good father to our children. He had a good job at Kraft Foods as the head of their computer tech department, and every day, he would tell me that he loved me. This was more than when I was growing up; it felt good.

I also had a new job, working downtown for the Veterans Hospital as an admission clerk on the night shift. On the other hand, grandmother was getting weaker, and she showed signs of dementia, which made it hard to care for her. I didn't know anything about this disabling condition, so when I took her to the doctor, they gave me reading material to help me understand and how to care for her. She had lost her sense of taste, and her appetite was decreasing; she was hardly eating to being with, and she liked crackers and herbal tea. Sometimes, I would try to get her some oatmeal, but she only ate a bit. I would be worried each time I went to work, wondering if she was ok with the girls and my guy since she was only used to me being around to care for her and the new apartment was very small.

The time came for me to do my two-week obligation for the Reserves, and they sent me to Wisconsin to write up training maps for recruits. The Job wasn't a problem because I was good with maps. The training outline had a starting point in the woods and diagrams throughout the map that would lead them to the next checkpoint on the map. I never had to work late, so when I got off, I would run on the post; I never left the post because I wasn't familiar with the area. The post had everything I needed: a small commissary to buy snacks and the Mess Hall for breakfast, lunch, and dinner. I also stayed in the barracks with one other female doing her two-week training. On Friday, a club was on the post with drinks, socializing, and dancing, but this was only for those in higher ranks than me. One Spanish sergeant would come around while I was working, trying to me but didn't need any help, but he wasn't a pest.

Chapter 13

Near death experience

My assignment was almost over, with one week to finish, and I was anxious to go back home to see my girls and check on my grandmother. The sergeant who always wanted to help would come to the barracks and ask if I wanted to run the track with him. Sometimes, I said yes, and sometimes, I didn't feel like running because I didn't have to. I only did it to keep in shape.

He seemed harmless, and I wasn't attracted to him at all, and I didn't think he liked me that way. When he did come around, even at the job site, he sat around reading his Bible and was good at quoting scripture. I was impressed with his knowledge of the Bible; I needed to start understanding the Word better for myself.

The time had finally come for me to pack up and get ready to go home. I considered the Sergeant my friend and trusted him. So, when he came to the barracks and offered to take me to the airport, I didn't think twice about it. I wasn't leaving till the next day, but he said I could spend the night at the hotel near the airport, which would be more confident than leaving after the same day as my flights. It sounded like a great idea; I won't have to wake up early since I wouldn't be far from the airport.

I put my duffle bag in the military truck, and he drove me to the Holiday Inn, which was, like he said, less than 2 miles away from the airport. I was excited to go home again. When we arrived at the hotel, he checked me in and volunteered to carry my bag to the room, but I told him I had it; he insisted, so I let him carry it to the door and said thanks. He entered my room without invitation and locked my door when my hotel room was open. I told him I was good and no longer needed his help. I knew right away something was very right, and I had been set up.

I was scared and didn't know what to do. I couldn't use the room phone while he looked at me. I knew I could never unlock the door and run out without him dragging me away.

My mind was blank. All the basic training I had received didn't help me that day. I accepted my fate; I was thick of it now.

Before I could scream, he knocked me to the bed with one hand over my mouth and the other hand pulling and jerking my pants down far enough where he had access to assault me. He had a crazy look in his eyes that I had never seen in him before. I felt his breath on me as tears rolled down my face in silence. I thought that if I fought him, I might not make it home tomorrow, so I just lay there and let him have his way. Finally, he was finished, I thought. When he got off me, he was sweating and had the nerve to apologize for what he just did to me, and that was enough. His exact words were, "I don't know what came over me, and I'm sorry." I just wanted him to leave so I could lock the door behind him, but he had other plans for me. He told me to take a shower and leave the door open. I didn't say a word; I just did what he said. After my shower, he asked me if I was hungry; I thought to myself, this man is crazy, and he's going to kill me. He was talking to me like nothing had ever happened, and it didn't matter to him that I didn't answer his stupid question about what I wanted to eat.

He ordered Pizza and insisted I eat with him. It was getting dark outside, and I was hoping he would leave; I told him I promised not to tell anyone what happened. But he told me he would be taking me to the airport tomorrow. I sat on the edge of the bed with tears running down my face, my head was pounding, and my heart was racing. I was stuck in a nightmare that I may never recover from. I could sleep out of fear; if he was planning to kill me, I wanted it to be quick, even though I swore to him I would never tell he didn't believe me and assaulted me again this time with a knife to my throat and kept saying how it felt. When he finished this time, he said, "I know you won't tell because you liked it." I wanted to die at that point. I was numb; I just curled up on the edge of the bed while he stayed up and watched television.

The morning finally came, and I prayed he would let me go home to my family. He woke like nothing had happened the night before and drove me to the airport. There, military police were present at the terminal, and I thought I would have him arrested as soon as I got to the terminal. But he must have done this before because he walked me to the terminal and talked to me like we were a couple.

When I was violated as a child, I was helpless, but now I'm grown up and still feel powerless. I was so ashamed and mentally messed up that when I was able to board the plane, I was still afraid. I kept this near-death experience to myself for years.

When I got off the plane, my guy was waiting for me; I had never been so glad to see him. I couldn't wait to get home and see grandmother and the girls. Once I looked at my beautiful girls, I felt everything would be ok. I thought about what my guy said about what would happen if I said no to his last proposal, so when he surprised me by asking if I would be his wife at the John Hancock building for dinner, I said yes. I've been searching for love when I should've loved me first.

I was about to learn all marriages aren't made in heaven.

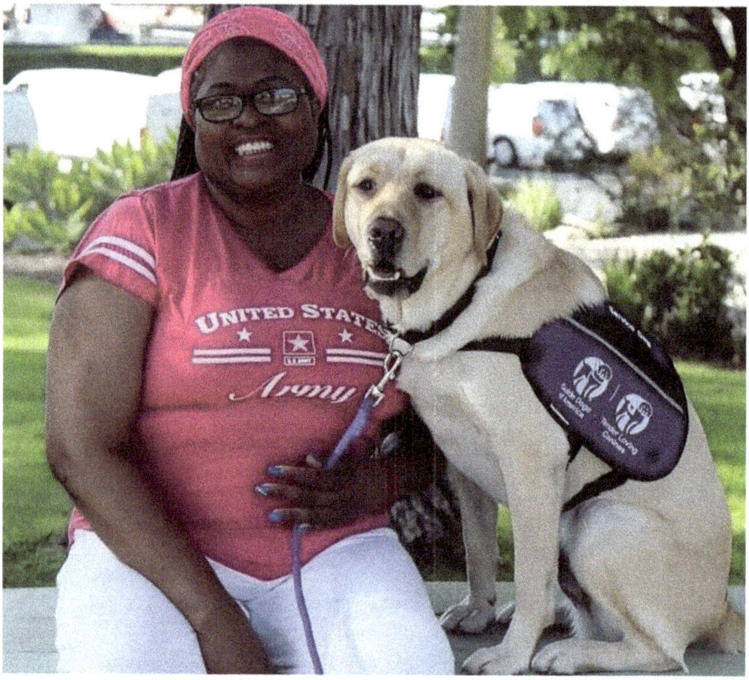
UNITED STATES
Army